O9-ABI-805

WEST GA REG LIB SYS
Neva Lomason
Memorial Library

DISCARD

First Facts

American Symbols

The Pledge of Allegiance

by Marc Tyler Nobleman

Consultant:
Melodie Andrews, Ph.D.
Associate Professor of Early American History
Minnesota State University, Mankato

Capstone
press

Capstone Press
151 Good Counsel Drive, P.O. Box 669, Mankato, Minnesota 56002
http://www.capstone-press.com

Copyright © 2003 by Capstone Press. All rights reserved.
No part of this publication may be reproduced in whole or in part, or stored in a retrieval system, or transmitted in any form or by any means, electronic, mechanical, photocopying, recording, or otherwise, without written permission of the publisher.
For information regarding permission, write to Capstone Press,
151 Good Counsel Drive, P.O. Box 669, Dept. R, Mankato, Minnesota 56002.
Printed in the United States of America

Library of Congress Cataloging-in-Publication Data
Nobleman, Marc Tyler.
    The Pledge of Allegiance / by Marc Tyler Nobleman.
    p. cm.—(American symbols)
    Summary: A simple introduction to the Pledge of Allegiance, discussing how it was written, modifications made over the years, its inclusion in the U.S. Flag Code, and more.
    Includes bibliographical references and index.
    ISBN 0-7368-1631-3 (hardcover)
    1. Bellamy, Francis. Pledge of Allegiance to the Flag—History—Juvenile literature.
2. Flags—United States—History—Juvenile literature. [1. Pledge of Allegiance] I. Title.
II. American symbols (Mankato, Minn.)
JK1759 .N63 2003
323.6'5'0973—dc21   2002010711

Editorial Credits
Chris Harbo and Roberta Schmidt, editors; Eric Kudalis, product planning editor;
    Linda Clavel, cover and interior designer; Alta Schaffer, photo researcher

Photo Credits
Capstone Press/Gary Sundermeyer, cover, 19, 21; Jim Foell, 5
Corbis/Bettmann, 7; Hulton-Deutsch Collection, 12; AFP, 15
Library of Congress, 13, 20
Rome Historical Society, 8
Watertown Free Public Library, 11

1 2 3 4 5 6 08 07 06 05 04 03

Table of Contents

Pledge of Allegiance Fast Facts 4

American Symbol of Loyalty 6

Francis Bellamy 8

A Pledge for Columbus Day 10

The Pledge Becomes a Tradition 12

The Pledge and the Flag Code 14

Changes to the Pledge of Allegiance 16

Saying the Pledge of Allegiance 18

Timeline 20

Hands On: Pledge Matching Game 22

Words to Know 23

Read More 24

Internet Sites 24

Index 24

Pledge of Allegiance Fast Facts

- Francis Bellamy wrote the Pledge of Allegiance in 1892.

- Students first said the Pledge of Allegiance on Columbus Day, 1892. This day celebrated the 400th anniversary of Christopher Columbus' arrival to the Americas.

- Bellamy's version of the Pledge of Allegiance had 23 words. Today, the pledge has 31 words.

- In 1943, the Supreme Court ruled that schools could not force children to say the pledge.

- President Dwight D. Eisenhower asked Congress to add the words "under God" to the Pledge of Allegiance in 1954.

- People stand, look at the flag, and hold their right hands over their hearts when they say the pledge.

American Symbol of Loyalty

The Pledge of Allegiance is a symbol of loyalty to the United States. People say the pledge to show respect for their country. The pledge is not a law. Americans do not have to say the Pledge of Allegiance.

loyalty
faithfulness to a person, place, or idea

Francis Bellamy

Francis Bellamy wrote the Pledge of Allegiance in 1892. He was the editor of the *Youth's Companion* magazine in Boston.

editor
a person who gets books, magazines, and newspapers ready for people to read

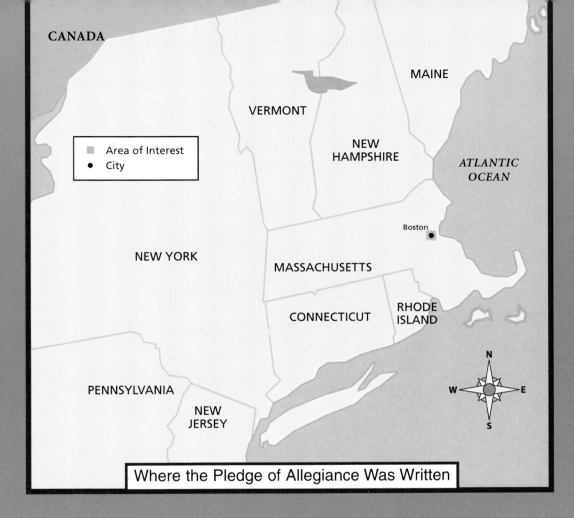

Where the Pledge of Allegiance Was Written

This magazine was popular with school children. It printed the pledge on September 8, 1892.

A Pledge for Columbus Day

Bellamy wanted students to say the pledge on Columbus Day in 1892. This day celebrated the 400th anniversary of Christopher Columbus reaching the Americas. Bellamy mailed copies of the Pledge of Allegiance to schools around the country.

anniversary

a day people remember every year because something important happened on that date in the past

The Pledge Becomes a Tradition

Millions of children said the Pledge of
Allegiance on Columbus Day. Students
and teachers liked the pledge.

Children started to say the pledge every day. It became a tradition in schools around the country.

tradition
a practice continued over many years

The Pledge and the Flag Code

In 1942, Congress added the pledge to the U.S. Flag Code. This list of rules helps people use the American flag correctly. The code has rules for saying the pledge. People should take off their hats when they say the pledge. Soldiers should salute the flag during the pledge.

15

The Pledge in 1892

**I pledge allegiance
to my flag
and to the Republic
for which it stands,
one Nation indivisible,
with liberty and
justice for all.**

The Pledge of Allegiance has changed twice since 1892. In 1923, the words "my flag" were changed to "the flag of the United States of America."

The Pledge Today

**I pledge allegiance
to the flag
of the United States of America
and to the Republic
for which it stands,
one Nation under God,
indivisible, with liberty
and justice for all.**

In 1954, President Dwight D. Eisenhower asked Congress to change the pledge again. Congress added the words "under God" after the word "nation."

Saying the Pledge of Allegiance

People can say the Pledge of Allegiance anytime. Children often say the pledge in school. They stand to say the pledge. They face the American flag. They put their right hands over their hearts.

Timeline

1892—Francis Bellamy writes the Pledge of Allegiance.

1892—Students recite the Pledge of Allegiance for the first time on Columbus Day.

1923—The words "my flag" are changed to "the flag of the United States of America."

1942—The U.S. government adds the Pledge of Allegiance to the Flag Code.

1992—The Pledge of Allegiance has its 100-year anniversary.

1954—Congress adds the words "under God" to the Pledge of Allegiance.

Hands On: Pledge Matching Game

Make a matching game using words from the Pledge of
Allegiance. This game will help you learn the meanings
of the words in the pledge.

What You Need

12 index cards
Pencil
Words to Know list on page 23
Two or more friends

What You Do

1. Write each of the following words on its own index card:
   pledge, allegiance, republic, indivisible, liberty, justice.
2. Find the meaning of each word in the Words to Know list
   on page 23. Write the meaning of each word on its own
   index card.
3. Mix the 12 cards together.
4. Put the cards facedown on a desk or on the floor. Make
   sure you cannot see the writing.
5. With friends, take turns turning over two cards. Try to
   find a match between a word and its meaning.
6. If you find a match, keep the two cards. If you do not
   find a match, turn the two cards facedown again.
7. The winner is the person who finds the most matches.

Words to Know

allegiance (uh-LEE-junss)—loyal support for something

Congress (KONG-griss)—the branch of the U.S. government that makes laws

indivisible (in-duh-VIZ-uh-buhl)—unable to be broken

justice (JUHSS-tiss)—fair treatment or behavior

liberty (LIB-ur-tee)—freedom

pledge (PLEJ)—to make a promise

republic (ri-PUHB-lik)—a government run by elected officials

soldier (SOLE-jur)—someone who is in the military

symbol (SIM-buhl)—an object that stands for something else

Read More

Schaefer, Lola M. *The Pledge of Allegiance.* Symbols of Freedom. Chicago: Heinemann Library, 2002.

Swanson, June. *I Pledge Allegiance.* On My Own History. Minneapolis: Carolrhoda Books, 2002.

Internet Sites

Track down many sites about the Pledge of Allegiance.

Visit the FACT HOUND at
http://www.facthound.com

IT IS EASY! IT IS FUN!

1) Go to *http://www.facthound.com*
2) Type in: 0736816313
3) Click on "FETCH IT" and FACT HOUND
   will find several links hand-picked by our editors.

Relax and let our pal FACT HOUND do the research for you!

Index

Bellamy, Francis, 8, 10
children, 9, 12, 13, 18
Columbus, Christopher, 10
Columbus Day, 10
Congress, 14, 17
Eisenhower, Dwight D., 17

flag, 14, 16, 18
Flag Code, 14
loyalty, 6
salute, 14
soldiers, 14
Youth's Companion, 8

The Pledge of allegiance /
J 323.65 NOBLE   31057001486961

Nobleman, Marc Tyler.
WEST GA REGIONAL LIBRARY SYS